A diamond in its natural state

Diamonds

Peter Murray

A⁺

Smart Apple Media

COPYRIGHT

☼ Published by Smart Apple Media

1980 Lookout Drive, North Mankato, MN 56003

Designed by Rita Marshall

Copyright © 2002 Smart Apple Media. International copyright reserved in
all countries. No part of this book may be reproduced in any form without
written permission from the publisher.

Printed in the United States of America

☼ Photographs by Archive Photos (Lambert, Reuters/The Smithsonian),
Anne Gordon, JLM Visuals (Breck Kent), Tom Myers, Tom Stack & Associates
(Therisa Stack, Tom Stack), Unicorn Stock Photos (Paul Hein)

☼ Library of Congress Cataloging-in-Publication Data

Murray, Peter. Diamonds / by Peter Murray. p. cm. — (From the earth)

Includes bibliographical references and index.

☼ ISBN 1-58340-111-3

1. Diamonds—Juvenile literature. [1. Diamonds.] I. Title. II. Series.

TN990 .M57 2001   553.8'2—dc21   00-069819

☼ First Edition 9 8 7 6 5 4 3 2 1

Diamonds

Brilliant Beginnings

It was a long, long time ago. The seas were warm and cloudy with the first primitive life-forms. The planet Earth was young. ☼ One hundred miles (160 km) beneath the surface, a mixture of molten rocks and metals, called **magma**, churned under tremendous heat and pressure. Pockets of pure carbon were squeezed into hard, eight-sided **crystals**. Most of these crystals were as tiny as grains of sand, but a few were much, much larger. ☼ The pressure built. When a weakness

---

Diamonds are formed by intense heat and pressure

appeared in the planet's crust, this mixture of carbon crystals

and molten rock was forced up through miles of crust. It broke

through, spilling its treasure onto the surface. ☀ Three

billion years later, early humans found some **Graphite, coal, soot, and diamonds are all forms of carbon.**

of these carbon crystals in riverbeds. They

had never seen a rock so hard. No one knew

where the rocks had come from. Had they fallen from the sky?

Were they formed by lightning bolts? ☀ In India, the stones

were called *vajra*, meaning "thunderbolt." The ancient Greeks

Coal, like diamonds, is made from carbon

A large diamond mine in Africa

called the stones *adamas*, meaning "invincible." ☀ Today,

we call them diamonds.

From Dull to Sparkling

Diamonds in their natural state, fresh from the earth,

are not very pretty. **Rough diamonds** look like chunks of

dull, grayish glass. Diamonds are the hardest natural substance

known. A diamond will easily scratch glass, metals, and rocks.

Originally, diamonds were believed to have magical powers.

They were stored in royal treasuries and not used as jewelry.

☀ During the Middle Ages (700–1500 A.D.), jewelers learned

how to cut and polish diamonds. When diamonds are **faceted**

and polished, they become beautiful, sparkling **gems**. ☀ For

thousands of years, diamonds were considered too rare and

A diamond in the rough

luxurious for common folk. Only kings, queens, and other royalty were allowed to own them. Later, in the 1400s, diamonds became more common and were worn by anyone who could afford them.

Famous Diamonds

The largest diamond ever found was about the size of a baking potato and weighed 3,106 carats. The stone was named the Cullinan, after the president of the mining company. The Cullinan diamond was not only enormous, it was nearly **flawless**. ☀ After studying the huge rough diamond for

months, a famous diamond cutter named Joseph Asscher cut

the stone into nine large diamonds and 96 smaller stones.

The biggest stone, named the Great Star of Africa, weighed

The Hope Diamond is said to be cursed

530 carats. It was set into the British Royal Scepter, where it remains to this day. ☼ One of the oldest and most famous diamonds is the Koh-i-noor, which means "mountain of light."

According to legend, the 800-carat diamond was set into the royal crown of India 5,000 years ago. In the 1300s, the Koh-i-noor was cut into a smaller stone weighing 186 carats. Over the next 600 years, many of those who owned the Koh-i-noor were murdered. The stone seemed to bring bad luck to all who

One carat is equal to 200 milligrams, or 141 carats per ounce.

Royalty often adorn crowns with diamonds

possessed it. In 1849, the stone was presented to Queen

Victoria of Britain. Because the diamond was poorly cut, the

queen had it recut to a smaller size. The Koh-i-noor was then

set into the crown of Queen Elizabeth. It is now on display

with the British royal jewels in the Tower of London.

"Will You Marry Me?"

As recently as a few hundred years ago, no one had

ever heard of a diamond engagement ring. Sometime during

the late 1800s, the custom of a man giving one to his true love

began. In the United States, three out of every four brides

receive diamond engagement rings. Diamond engagement

rings are also popular in Europe and Japan. ☀ Fewer than

one-fifth of all diamonds are gem quality, however. Most

A typical engagement ring is one carat in size

diamonds are very small, discolored, and not good enough to

be used for jewelry. These lower-quality diamonds are used in

industry on saw blades and drill bits to cut **Diamonds**
are so hard
through concrete and other hard substances. **they can**
be polished
Diamond-tipped drill bits are used to drill deep **only with**
diamond
into the earth for oil. Diamond dust is used to **dust.**

polish lenses, gems, hard metals—even dental fillings. As useful

as they are beautiful, diamonds will always be one of our most

treasured minerals.

Diamond certificates detail a stone's quality

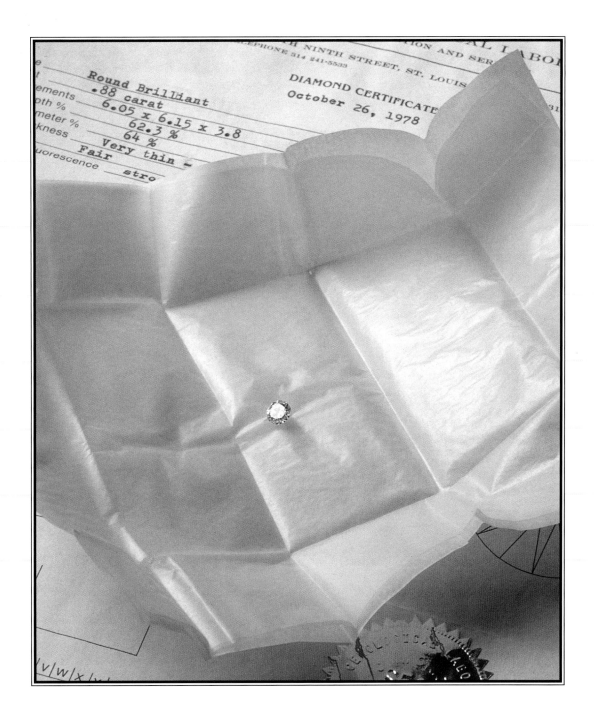

Learning About Crystals

What You Need

A magnifying glass

Table salt

White sugar

What You Do

1. Look carefully at a few grains of salt through the magnifying glass.

2. Now look at the sugar. How are the sugar crystals different from the salt crystals?

What You See

Salt forms even, six-sided crystals. Each grain of salt is like a tiny square box. Sugar forms oblong crystals. Different minerals form differently shaped crystals. Diamonds form eight-sided crystals that look like two pyramids with their bases stuck together.

This diamond has 58 facets, or sides

INFORMATION

Index

Words to Know

crystals (KRIS-tuls)—transparent minerals that break apart, leaving flat, smooth surfaces

faceted (FAS-eh-ted)—gems cut to form flat surfaces

flawless (FLAW-less)—perfect in every way

gems (JEMS)—decorative stones valued for their beauty and rarity

magma (MAG-muh)—the semi-molten mixture of rocks and metals found beneath the earth's crust

rough diamonds (RUFF DIE-munds)—diamonds in their natural state

Read More

Harlow, George E., ed. *The Nature of Diamonds*. Cambridge, Mass.: Cambridge University Press, 1997.

Milne, Jean. *The Story of Diamonds*. North Haven, Conn.: Linnet Books, 2000.

Symes, R. F. *Rocks and Minerals*. New York: Knopf, 1988.

Internet Sites

Rockhounds with Rocky

http://www.fi.edu/fellows/payton/rocks/index2.html

Ask-a-Geologist

http://walrus.wr.usgs.gov/docs/ask-a-ge.html/

The Mineral and Gemstone Kingdom

http://www.minerals.net